THE
OUTDOOR
GARDEN
ROOM

THE
OUTDOOR
GARDEN
ROOM

25 PROJECTS FOR
STYLISH SUMMER LIVING

DEBORAH SCHNEEBELI-MORRELL

NORTH LIGHT BOOKS
Cincinnati, Ohio

DEDICATION

For Nan Farquharson who has helped me more than she knows

First published in North America
in 2001 by North Light Books
an imprint of F&W Publications, Inc.
1507 Dana Avenue
Cincinnati, OH 45207
1-800/289-0963

ISBN 1-58180-219-6

First published in 2001 by Cico Books Ltd
32 Great Sutton Street London EC1V 0NB

Edited by Gillian Haslam
Photography by Heini Schneebeli
Styling by Deborah Schneebeli-Morrell
Designed by David Fordham

Reproduction by Master Image Pte Ltd, Singapore
Typeset by Mats, Southend-on-Sea, Essex
Printed and bound in Singapore by Tien Wah Press

CONTENTS

INTRODUCTION

A GARDEN IS A PLACE FOR LIVING just as much as the inside of the home; it is where we play, rest, work, and dream. For those of us who love gardening, it is the most rewarding and therapeutic place in the world and, most importantly, a place that inspires our creativity. This creativity allows us to enhance our lives and those of our friends and families.

Most people like to encourage wildlife or small birds to the garden. In winter they can drink from the pretty mosaic birdbath made from china shards, and in summer we may be lucky enough to see them splash around in the water. A bird table or feeder is also a must. Being so engaged with the natural world creates an opportunity to enjoy our environment; it is quite fascinating to watch and identify all the feathered visitors. However, the gardener's life is not all rosy. Pests, greedy rabbits, and devouring birds can destroy a crop in a very short time – action must be taken to discourage such unwelcome marauders. By following old country traditions, you can create scarecrows and bird scarers; the projects in this book show you how to make them functional as well as a decorative feature in themselves.

The garden in summer, however large or small, can be transformed into another room. We all welcome the opportunity to spend so much time outside; we feel healthier, more optimistic, and more sociable. Everything seems easier and, with the wonderful background of an abundant and flourishing garden, what better place to entertain? You can make a table for day or night-time entertaining; for special occasions, you can make stunning little lanterns so easily from nothing but small glass jars and a little wire. The lovely paper bag lanterns could not be easier to make. You may like to make a slightly more adventurous project, such as the beautiful sturdy garden gate; use it to divide your garden into areas, or to draw the eye to a focal point in the distance, a well known garden designers' trick. Making mosaics for outside is easy to do so long as you use knee-pads for comfort and have the patience required for sorting all those pebbles. Follow the instructions for the pebble mosaic and you may be inspired to create a much larger feature, such as a path or sun terrace. For some-thing quick and simple, try the painted flowerpots and transform an everyday clay pot with a striking pattern. In fact, this whole book is about using materials in an imaginative way and transforming and adapting them to make unique and functional objects. Enhance and decorate your garden, reaping pleasures and rewards just as you do in your home.

NOTE ON MEASUREMENTS: The measurements for each of the projects in the book are given both in metric and imperial quantities. Once you have decided which system to use, do follow it through the project, as the measurements are not interchangeable.

PEBBLE
MOSAIC

MANY PEOPLE COLLECT pebbles while away on vacation, while at the beach, by a lakeside, or up in the mountains. There is something about their color and shape, and where and when they were found, which seems almost magically to embody the sense or spirit of a place. One sees them in homes, arranged in bowls or spaced along a shelf or windowsill, even strewn in a garden, each one carrying a silent story. How much more rewarding to make your own pebble mosaic, incorporating those precious "found" stones with others that can be bought in bulk to make an original and permanent design. The quantities given in the list of materials are necessarily vague – how much you need depends how large you wish your panel to be. Just make sure you use the correct ratio of sand to cement (see step 3 overleaf).

MATERIALS

Aggregate

Garden rake

Sack of medium-sized river pebbles (pick out gray and four large black ones)

Sack of small white river pebbles

Sack of small brown/purple river pebbles

Sack of purple/black slate pieces

Water hose

Sharp sand

Cement

Spade

Bricklayer's float

Sharp pointed stick

Small brush

LEFT AND RIGHT: This effective mosaic panel is ideal for the beginner as it is based on a very simple geometric design. It is not difficult to make – you just require patience and kneepads!

HOW TO MAKE A PEBBLE MOSAIC

1 Fill the area chosen for the mosaic with aggregate to a depth of 4in (10cm) to make a firm base. Rake it level and tread it down. The finished mosaic (pebbles and mortar) will be approximately 2½ in (6cm) deep, so make allowance for this depth on top of the aggregate base.

2 Sort out the pebbles and slate. You will need to pick out evenly sized examples (often up to half will need to be discarded). Have a container of large gray pebbles, one of smaller white ones, and another of small brown/ purple ones. Sort out a smaller number of the slate pieces. Wash them all thoroughly with the water hose.

3 Mix two parts sand to one part cement and fill in the area on top of the aggregate to a depth of approximately 2½ in (6cm). Firm and level this dry mortar layer with a bricklayer's float.

4 Using a sharp pointed stick (a long paintbrush handle or a chopstick will do), draw your chosen design into the dry mortar. The outer border needs to be wide enough to accommodate three rows of the larger pebbles. Mark a diamond within the rectangle and a circle within the diamond (the precise design and measurements will depend on the size of pebbles you are using).

5 Push three rows of the larger gray pebbles into the mortar mix to at least half their depth to make the border. Use them lengthwise, on their sides, with the narrowest edge facing up.

6 Draw an eight-pointed star in the central circle and push in pieces of slate, thin edges facing up. You will need two or three per point, but try to use narrow pieces.

7 Push small white pebbles into the spaces between the slate lines, choosing them carefully so the star keeps its shape. Make sure that the edge of the circle is even.

Use the small brown/purple pebbles to surround the central motif, arranging them neatly in a concentric pattern. Fill in the whole diamond area in this way, pushing the pebbles into the mortar. You can tamp them down with the bricklayer's float to create a really even top surface.

Choose a large black pebble and lay it flat side up in the center of the remaining triangular spaces. Fill in the remaining spaces with the white pebbles.

Add a couple of shovels of the dry mortar mix to the surface to fill in and even out the mortar base. Brush off the excess and remove. Spray the finished mosaic with a fine mist from the water hose for a couple of minutes to dampen the surface.

TIP The mortar can take up to a month to cure, so avoid walking on the mosaic until it is firmly set.

VEGETABLE
ROW MARKERS

THESE PRETTY TWISTED WIRE and aluminum seed row markers are both practical and decorative, and this simple and inexpensive project may even be made from found or recycled materials. When sowing seeds, it is important to mark the rows, so that you know where the seedling plants will emerge. This means you will neither inadvertently oversow one row with another, nor mistake the seedlings for weeds. As the plants grow up, the markers are tall enough to be read above the foliage.

MATERIALS
4½ yards (4m) galvanized wire,
1/16in (1mm) thick
Wooden spoon
Wirecutters
Bent-nosed pliers
Dressmaker's tracing wheel
Strong scissors
Protective gloves
Card template
Piece of aluminum, 12 x 8in (30 x 20cm),
½in (0.5mm) thick
Indelible black marker pen

LEFT AND ABOVE: Remember to use an indelible pen to inscribe the variety of the seeds sown, and this ink will survive in all weathers.

HOW TO MAKE VEGETABLE ROW MARKERS

1 Twist the wire by looping it around a fixed point such as a table leg. Wind the ends around the spoon handle and twist tightly together. Keep turning the handle until the entire length is twisted. Use wirecutters to cut the wire from the fixed point and the spoon.

2 Bend the twisted wire in half, creating a heart shape at the midway point. Then twist the two lengths together tightly where they cross at the base of the heart.

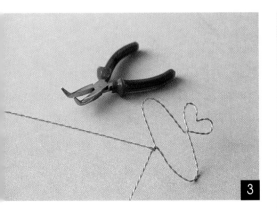

3 Form the two lengths into an oval shape measuring 4½in (11cm) at the widest point, then bring them back together and twist to join them. Hold this point tightly with the pliers and twist the two lengths together until the stem is 10in (25cm) long. Leave the rest untwisted.

4 Open out the two lengths of twisted wire so they are 2in (5cm) apart and curve out from the central stem. Cut off excess wire so the twisted foot measures 6in (15cm).

5 Cut out a template from a scrap of card. Draw around the template onto the aluminum with a black pen, and cut out the shape with strong scissors. (You may wish to wear protective gloves as the metal can be sharp.)

6 Use the tracing wheel to create a bumpy line all around the edge of the metal. You will need to press quite hard to make an impression – it may be easier to rest the metal on a yielding surface, such as a telephone directory.

7 Lay the wire oval over the aluminum and bend up the tabs on the metal so they grip the wire frame securely. Write the name of the plant on the other side of the marker.

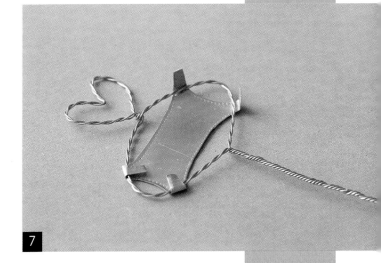

W I R E
SHELVES

OBJECTS FOR THE GARDEN made from wire were once much more common than they are today, and are now often collected as antiques. Although they were usually made by light industrial processes, many designs can be made by hand. Look at old examples, such as egg or potato baskets, work out the technique, and try to re-create one for yourself – it is easier than you think. This little wirework shelf is both useful and decorative and can be made from scraps of leftover wire. As it is made from aluminum and galvanized chicken wire, it is suitable for outdoor use. Fixed to a shed or porch wall, it makes an ideal place for storing essential garden items such as garden clippers, small tools, or balls of twine so they can be found again easily. How many pairs of pruners have been lost in undergrowth or swept up onto a compost heap, only to be found a year later, rusted and beyond use?

RIGHT: The decorative spiral edge around the sides of these shelves, simply made into loops with your fingers, turns an everyday item into something special.

LEFT: The perfect storage solution for the keen gardener – open wirework shelves just the right size for holding secateurs and other small gardening tools.

MATERIALS

Approximately 6½ yards (6m) of ⅛in (3mm) thick aluminum wire
Wirecutters
Box file 13in x 10in x 3-4in (34 x 25 x 9cm)
Bent-nosed pliers
Small roll of galvanized wire ⅛in (1mm) thick for binding
Small gauge galvanized chicken wire approximately 20in x 2ft
(50cm x 60cm)

HOW TO MAKE WIRE SHELVES

1 Cut a 5ft (150cm) piece of the aluminum wire and bend it carefully around the box file as shown, leaving two ends of equal length at the top. Using the pliers, make a loop at one end, remove the box and bind the two ends together with thin binding wire so the loop is in the middle of the top. Cut off any excess wire from the unlooped end. This forms the back frame of the cupboard, with a hanging loop.

1

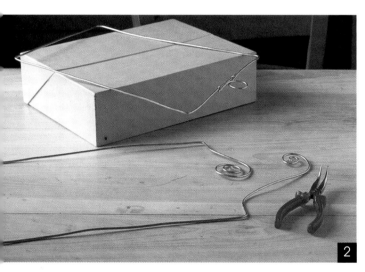

2

2 Cut a piece of aluminum wire 5½ft (170cm) long and bend it round the box file as before, leaving two equal lengths at the top. On each side, ¾in (2cm) in from the top corners, bend the remaining wire into large inward-turning spirals. Where the spirals touch at the center, bind together with thin binding wire. This forms the front frame of the shelf.

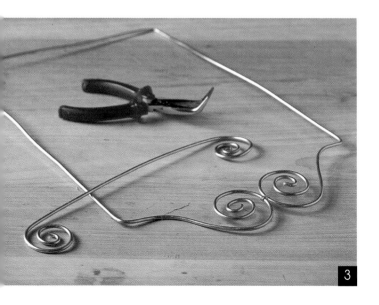

3

3 Cut a 1ft 8in (50cm) length of the aluminum wire and twist each end into a spiral, leaving the straight edge approximately the same length as the width of the previously made frames.

4 Lay this new piece across the top of the front frame, spirals facing upward, and bind it to secure it in position with the binding wire in four places – at each end and at the point where the frame spirals touch the straight length of the shorter piece.

5 Lay the box file centrally on the chicken wire and use the wirecutters to cut out each corner square as shown. Allow an extra margin of ½in (1cm) on each side, which will make the corners easier to secure. Bend the chicken wire up on each side and cut level with the top of the box.

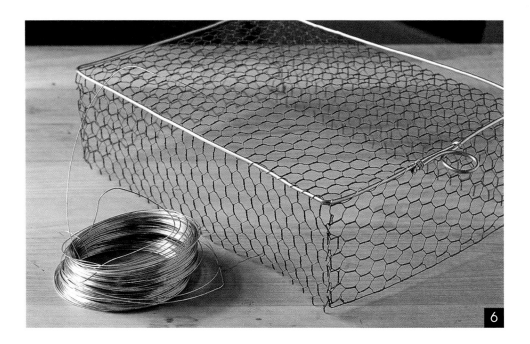

6 Remove the box file and bend the wire ends of the overlapping corners over each other to make a firm join. The chicken wire should now form a sturdy box. Lay the back aluminum frame onto the back of the box, making sure the frame corresponds exactly with the corners. Secure it in place by binding it with the binding wire.

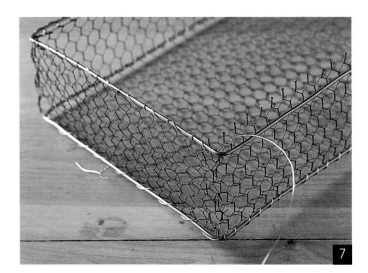

7 Turn the box over and bind the front decorative frame to the chicken wire in the same manner. Use the pliers to turn under any sharp, protruding pieces of the cut edges of the chicken wire.

8 Make the shelf in the same way as the box and frame, making sure it is slightly smaller than the width and depth measurement of the box to enable it to fit in easily. Bind it in place into the middle of the box.

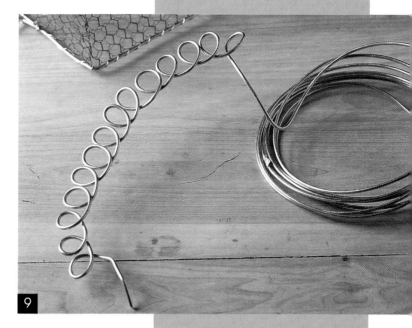

9 Use the remaining aluminum wire to make a length of small loops to use as the decorative border. This is easily done with the fingers – try to keep the loops flat and of an even size.

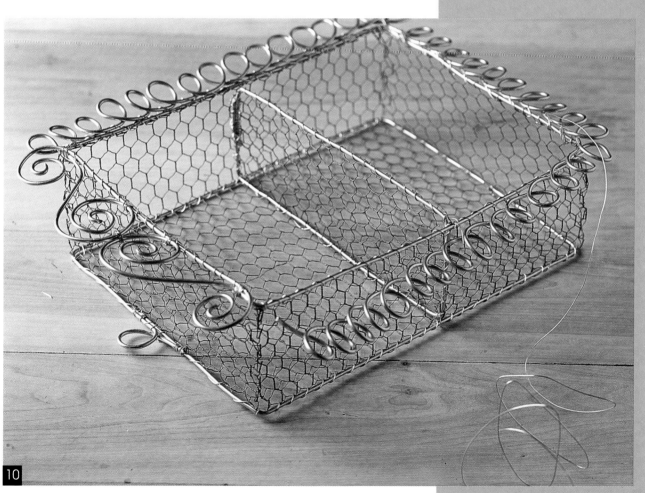

10 Secure the looped border to the front edge of the box by using the binding wire. Cut the wire into lengths of approximately 23in (50cm) to make it easier to manipulate.

W I R E
EGG BASKET

THIS DELICATE BASKET is actually rather strong and hardwearing. Its shiny galvanized wire and aluminum gauze will weather with age and eventually improve its appearance. It is the perfect size for collecting eggs, but could be used for any number of purposes. For instance, it would look pretty lined with moss and planted with spring bulbs such as snowdrops or grape hyacinths. The decorative and functional aspects of the basket, the loops and spirals and scrolls, are commonly used in traditional wirework and have been used in the wire shelves on page 18, the vegetable row markers on page 14, and the wire pot holders on page 86. The aluminum gauze used here is obtained from sculptors' suppliers and is normally used for making armatures, as it is incredibly soft and pliable. In this project, it is molded over a small mixing bowl, the flat sheet being pleated neatly in four places in order to make the body of the basket.

LEFT: This pretty basket is made by molding aluminum gauze around a mixing bowl. You could experiment by using different shaped bowls as molds and make baskets of all shapes and sizes.

MATERIALS

Small mixing bowl as mold, 7in (16cm) in diameter and 4in (10cm) high.

Jelly jar

Aluminum gauze, 12in (30cm) square

Scissors

Galvanized wire ½in (0.5mm) thickness, twisted double to make approximately 5½ yards (5m), (see glass jar lanterns, pages 92-95)

Small piece of single ½in (0.5mm) wire for binding

Wirecutters

4 clothes pins

Flat-ended modeling tool

Reel of fine jeweler's wire for binding

Pliers

12in (30cm) length of dowel, ¾in (1.5cm) in diameter

HOW TO MAKE A WIRE
EGG BASKET

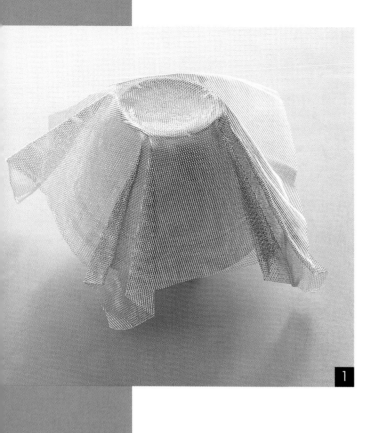

1 Place the bowl upside-down on a glass jar
   so that it does not touch the table. Place
the aluminum gauze on top, make a double
pleat at four equidistant places, and press it
into shape with your hands. Treat the aluminum
gauze as if you were pleating stiff material.

2 Turn the bowl the right
   way up and snip off all
the gauze that stands
beyond the rim.

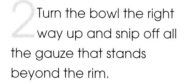

3 Cut a piece of twisted wire long enough
   to go around the top of the bowl, plus a
½in (1cm) overlap. Bind the wire circlet
together with the thicker of the binding wires,
finishing off the ends neatly.

4 Place this wire circlet around the outside of the basket, ½in (1cm) below the rim. Clothes pin it in place and turn the rim over, tucking it tightly under the twisted wire, and pushing it into place using the flat-ended modeling tool.

5 Cut two pieces of the twisted wire 24in (60cm) long and two 22in (55cm) long. Use the pliers to make spiral ends, each spiral facing the same way.

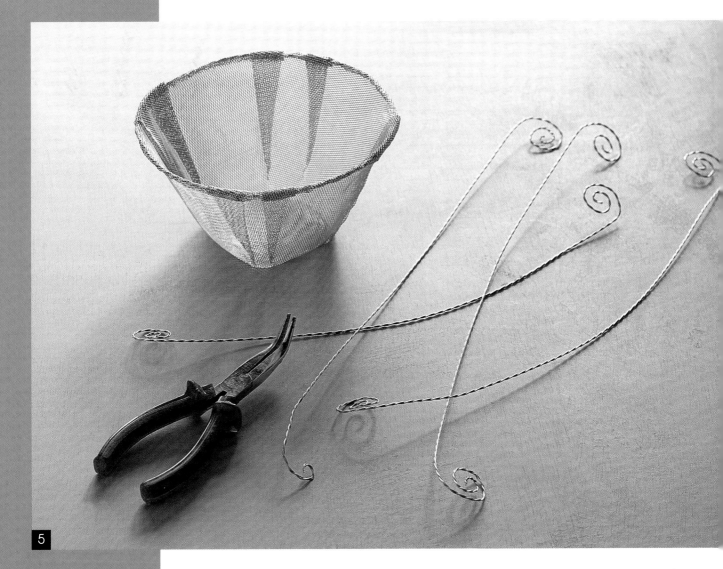

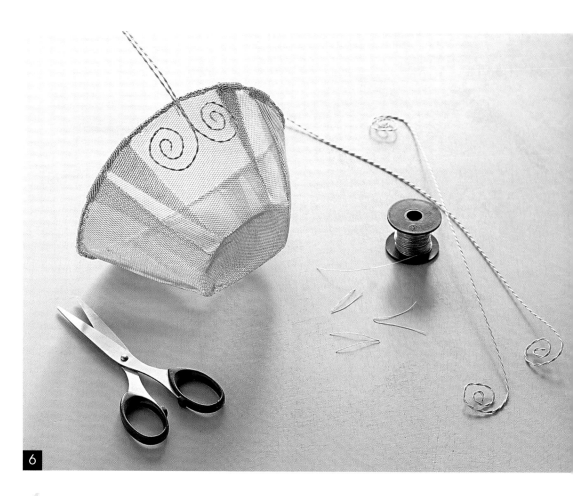

6 Lay the basket on its side and place the two longer spirals in a mirror image of the other one as shown. Attach them, using short pieces of the fine jeweler's wire (bent into "hairpins"). To hold the wire in place, push a "hairpin" through to the back and twist it tightly to secure the wire. Cut off the excess, leaving a short piece of the twist. Bend the wire over to make a handle and repeat the process on the other side.

7 Take the shorter pieces and place the spirals facing inward against the handle, just above the rim. Bind them together and make a double handle, using the fine wire, and binding onto the rim. Curve each length symmetrically inward and attach it to the handle 2½in (6cm) above the rim. Bend the remaining parts over and repeat on the other side of the basket, neatly binding together the four pieces at the center of the handle.

8 Wind 2 yards (2m) of the twisted wire around the dowel as tightly as possible, and remove and flatten the loops. You will need twelve loops either side of the handle.

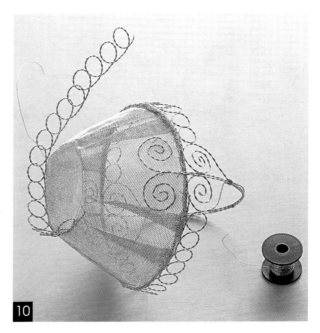

10 Attach a border of sixteen loops to the base in the same manner. This is a little more tricky since there is no wire rim to bind around. You will probably need to work with one hand inside the basket.

9 Start binding the looped border in place with the fine wire, binding the first loop to the spiral where it meets. When one side is complete, cut the border and start again on the other side, binding it in the same way.

PAPER BAG
LANTERNS

PROBABLY THE QUICKEST and most inexpensive project in this book, these stunningly effective lanterns add a magical touch to an evening garden party. Use them to light a pathway or to decorate a romantic seating area. Flat-bottomed paper bags are readily available; ask a friendly grocer to give or sell you as many as you think you might need. The bags may be secured at the sites you choose by filling the base with two cupfuls of sand. Place a long-lasting votive candle inside a glass jar for safety, then push the jar into the sand inside the bag. Make sure the bag's sides are upright and not folding inward, in order to protect them from the heat of the flame. After use, the bags can be emptied, then stored flat, ready for future use. Although they are only paper, proper care means that they will last a long time.

MATERIALS

Flat-bottomed paper
    bags approximately.
    10 x 14½in (25 x 37cm)
Card template
Fine pen
Small cutting mat
Craft knife
Sand
Votive candles
Glass jars

HOW TO MAKE PAPER BAG LANTERNS

1 Make your stencil from the template on the left. Cut out the leaf and stem shapes as shown. Lay the stencils onto the bag and draw through the holes, to transfer the design onto the bag, placing one leaf higher than the other.

2 Push the cutting mat between the two sides of the paper bag, making a suitable surface for cutting on, and protecting the back layer (which should not be cut).

3 Very carefully cut around the marked lines to reveal the cut–through leaf shapes. Try not to be too tentative. Use the knife as if you were drawing with a pencil, in order to obtain a confident, flowing line.

31

P U M P K I N
VASE

LEFT: This inventive vase is extremely practical, and you can choose the shape and size of pumpkin to suit the color and form of your flowers. Here a red kuri squash has been used.

MANY VARIETIES OF pumpkins and squashes are now available in grocery stores. For even more choice, grow your own from seed and watch them develop at an astonishing rate. They are wonderful to eat, whether baked in the oven with a good olive oil, or made into a spicy soup that is served in its own shell. They can be carved into lanterns for the festival of Halloween and make stunning still-life decorations (until you are tempted to eat them). This vase keeps flowers fresh for days, so long as you refill it with water intermittently, just as you would with any other vase. The clever device of having individual holes for each flower stem means you can create the shape you want, rather than have all the stems bunched up in the wrong place. This arrangement would enhance a harvest supper table or would make a wonderful centerpiece for a late summer lunch.

MATERIALS

Squash (choose one that balances well on its base)

Fine-tip marker pen

Small kitchen knife

Small gimlet (size depends on thickness of flower stems)

Jug for water

Bunch each of gerberas (pink, red, and orange), green poppy
   seedheads, and bells of Ireland (*Moluccella laevis*)

HOW TO MAKE A PUMPKIN VASE

1 Draw a circle around the stem – about 3in (7.5cm) in diameter. Cut around this line with the kitchen knife and remove the "lid." Set this aside as you will need it later.

2 Pull out all the seeds and stringy loose flesh from the inside using your fingers.

3 Use the gimlet to bore two rows of
equidistant holes around the cut-out
center. Bore four additional holes in the lid.

4 Pour in water, filling the squash up to just
below the lowest line of holes, and replace
the lid. Insert each stem, building up an evenly
spaced, pleasing arrangement.

S W E E T P E A
WIGWAMS

TRADITIONAL WIGWAMS, made either entirely from willow, or woven with bands of willow, are a must for every garden. They are surprisingly simple to make, and also one of the most practical structures you can provide for fast-growing climbing plants.

If the wood is left untreated, these wigwams will last only a couple of seasons, which is why they are most usually used to train annuals such as sweetpeas. To extend their life, simply spray them with a proprietary garden timber paint (these contain a preservative and come in a number of subtle garden shades).

By painting them, these lovely structures become more visible, adding height, a focal point, and architectural interest to your garden design or planting scheme and, when the color is chosen carefully, can add an unexpected contrast to offset the color of the rambling sweetpeas and other plants growing nearby.

You may be lucky enough to have a willow or hazel tree growing in your garden, from which you can cut the straight rods to be placed upright in the wigwams. However, it is best to buy a bundle of purpose-grown willow stems from which to weave the horizontal bands. Working with hazel and willow may inspire you to make more inventive garden structures such as fences, cloches, or a trellis or arbor.

LEFT: This twig wigwam was painted blue. It now creates drama, reflecting the blue of the sky on a summer day, or adding interest on a dull, cloudy one.

MATERIALS

12 willow or hazel rods, each approximately
    5ft (1.8m) long
Bundle of willow, each approximately
    4½ft (1.5m) long
Strong garden clippers or long-handled
    pruning shears
Spray paint for wood, suitable for outdoor use
Garden wire (optional)

HOW TO MAKE A WIGWAM

1 Cut the thickest ends of the willow or hazel rods with the clippers to make a sharp diagonal cut; these will form the base ends. Measure four 5ft 4in (160cm) long, and cut a diagonal at the top end. Cut the remaining eight rods in the same way, to a length of 4ft (1.2m).

2 Push two of the long rods into soft ground approximately 16in (40cm) apart so that they stand upright. Push in the other two long rods at right angles, to form four points on a circle in the ground. Push two shorter rods, evenly spaced, between two of the longer ones, then repeat on the other sides to form a complete circle of twelve rods.

3 Take two pieces of willow and insert them horizontally 14in (35cm) up from the ground on either side of one of the rods. Now weave them together around the upright rods, crossing them just before they cross each new rod. The thin, tapered ends should just about reach around to where you started. Start with another two willow lengths on the next rod. Continue in this manner all the way around.

4 Continue weaving in this way, making three bands. The top band should be about 8in (20cm) from the top of the short rods. As you weave, pull together the uprights to make the "wigwam" structure. It is a good idea to tuck or tie in the loose, thin ends of the willow. Make the structure neater by cutting off all the protruding ends.

5 Hold the four top rods together to wrap them around and tie them together with a single strip of willow (you may like to tie the ends with garden wire first, for extra security). To finish, spray all over with paint.

TIP Fresh willow is easy to use and very pliable. If, however, it has dried out or is old, it can be revived by soaking overnight in a bathtub of water.

M O S A I C
BIRDBATH

THIS ELEGANT BIRDBATH looks just as good in a formal setting as it does in a wild garden. The project cleverly combines a generously proportioned pale terra-cotta bowl with pretty discarded blue-and-white china shards.

You may have kept favorite pieces of family china over the years that have become chipped or cracked, and be unwilling to discard them for sentimental reasons. However, you can also buy old china very inexpensively, and many older patterns are full of charm and style, often dating back centuries. Useful and plentiful sources are second-hand shops, fleamarkets, and thrift stores.

Whatever your source of china, transforming it into a beautiful mosaic pattern will make an enduring and much admired object for your garden, not least by the feathered guests in your backyard.

LEFT: A classic combination of timeless blue-and-white china shards and sturdy terra-cotta results in an elegant mosaic birdbath to attract wildlife to your garden.

MATERIALS

Collection of blue-and-white china shards

Tile cutter

Gray waterproof cement-based adhesive

Old kitchen knife

Terra-cotta bowl, approx 18in (45cm)
    in diameter, 6in (15cm) deep

Pale gray waterproof cement-based tile
    grout

Plastic spatula

Clean, damp sponge

Old cloth

HOW TO MAKE A MOSAIC BIRDBATH

1 Using the tile cutters, cut any large pieces of china into smaller sections. Cut and save the rims of the plates, as you will need the smooth finished edges of these later. Tile cutters work best when they are used to grip the edge of the shard. Press very firmly and the china will break in the intended place. As a general rule, high-fired (fine) china is harder to cut, while low-fired (everyday) pieces break far more easily.

2 Mix the cement adhesive according to the instructions on the package. Use the kitchen knife to apply some adhesive to the center of the base of the bowl. Place the first china shard in the center and begin to add the others around this, piecing them together like a jigsaw puzzle. You may need to shape some of the pieces with the tile cutters for a closer fit. As the shards will not all be of a uniform thickness, you will need to even the level by applying more cement to the thinner pieces. This can be done by applying the cement directly to the back of the china.

3

3 Continue in the same manner, making the surface level and fitting the china shards as closely as possible. Use the tile cutters to match the curve around the base with the pieces on the sloped wall of the sides.

4 When you reach the top of the sides, use the pieces with the rims that you set aside earlier to match the inner lip of the bowl. Allow to dry overnight.

4

5 Mix the grout according to the package's instructions and spread it across the surface of the mosaic, pushing it well into the gaps with the plastic spatula. This needs to be done very thoroughly. Remove the excess grout with a damp sponge when all the gaps have been filled. Wipe the clean sponge around the terra-cotta rim to remove any stray grout. Leave it to dry.

6 Polish the whole surface vigorously with a clean, dry cloth. Allow the grout and cement a couple of days to dry thoroughly before filling the birdbath with water.

RIGHT: Traditional blue-and-white willow pattern china has been used to create an eye-catching mosaic for the garden.

GALVANIZED TUB
ROCK GARDEN

THE ATTRACTION OF the wide variety of old-style galvanized tubs, baths, and buckets on sale today is not just limited to their pretty silver-gray sheen and novel shapes and sizes, but also to their understated ability to work as a garden centerpiece. Our grandmothers or even our mothers would have used them for washing before plastic replaced everything. The tubs are now sold as garden antiques, commanding ridiculous prices, but many still exist in attics, cellars, and garden sheds. Pull them out and fill them with plants, then place them in the sunniest part of the garden. This rectangular tub has been planted with low-growing alpines, which seem to enjoy being warmed by the reflected heat from the tub's metal sides, which cool down rapidly when the sun goes down. Alpine plants are hardy and suitable for most climates.

MATERIALS

Galvanized tub – this one is approximately 20 x 14 x 10in
(50 x 35 x 25cm)
Scrubbing brush
Heavy hammer
Strong steel nail 4in (10cm) long
Small bucket of coarse gravel
35-liter bag of compost mixed with a bucket of garden soil and a
bucket of uncolored sharp sand
¼ bucket of tiny pebble chippings
Selection of flattish, irregular-shaped river stones
Approximately 8 small alpine plants (color-themed in pinks, whites,
and purples)

LEFT AND RIGHT: This project is perfect for a small patio garden. You could also try planting the tub with a selection of herbs and positioning it by the kitchen door to provide a ready supply of fresh herbs for cooking.

HOW TO MAKE A GALVANIZED TUB ROCK GARDEN

1 Wash the tub thoroughly with water from a waterhose. Any ingrained dirt can be scrubbed off with a stiff brush. Turn the tub upside down and punch a series of equidistant drainage holes in the base using the hammer and the long nail.

2 Turn the tub right-side up and fill it with coarse gravel to a depth of about 2in (5cm). This will allow free drainage, which is so important for alpine plants.

3 Now fill the tub with the soil/compost mixture – up to 2in (5cm) from the rim of the tub. Press it down firmly, retaining the same level. You may need to add more soil.

4 Now create a rock garden effect by positioning the plants and river stones. Put the largest plant in first at a front corner, arranging it to spill over the edge of the tub. Place a stone on either side of the plant, then plant the next space, adding more stones so that, when all is planted, little earth is visible. Try to make it look as natural as possible.

5 Fill in spaces between the stones with the pebble chippings. The stones and chippings will help to retain moisture and keep the roots cool on very hot days. They will also help to protect against frost in the winter.

STENCILED EGG
WREATH

THE EGG SHAPE IS PROBABLY the most perfect that occurs in the natural world, so one needs to respect this fact when decorating it. Any decoration should complement and work with its shape. The small leaves used here are carefully chosen to fit each size of egg and, being flexible, can be wrapped around the egg in a considered way. The different eggs – hen, duck, and goose – have differing shell colors and this affects the way the dye will take, adding subtle nuances of color to your overall design. Because the eggs are first blown, they will last indefinitely. To blow the eggs, pierce a small hole at each end and carefully drain out the contents. Patterned with leaves from your backyard and interspersed with small feathers, this wreath will endure as a lasting homage to the natural world. It could be displayed each Easter, perhaps on a front door like the traditional Christmas wreath.

MATERIALS

Selection of small fresh garden leaves

10 blown goose, duck, and hen eggs

One pair 10 denier pantyhose

Scissors

Natural red dye

Synthetic dye in purple and orange

Old saucepan

Spoon

1 yard (1m) galvanized wire (1mm) ⅟₁₆in
    thick

Wirecutters

10 wands of white feathers

20 small wispy feathers (pheasant
    feathers were used here)

Craft glue

LEFT: Patterned eggs,
threaded together on a
length of wire with wispy
feathers, create a delicate
and eyecatching wreath.

51

HOW TO MAKE A STENCILED EGG WREATH

1 Select the leaves that fit best onto each egg. Wet the surface of the shell, lay the leaf in place, and smooth with your fingers to encourage the leaf to follow the egg shape.

2 Carefully place the egg, with the leaf attached, into a length of the nylon pantyhose. Tie the length tightly at one end and cut off the other end, leaving enough hose to tie another firm knot. The aim is to get the nylon to pull very tightly across the egg, holding the leaf in place and in complete contact with the shell.

3 Mix about one handful of the natural red dye and the purple dye in water (quantity as specified on the package,) and bring it to the boil. Simmer the dye for ten minutes, then remove the pan from the heat. Place five eggs in the dye and hold them down with a spoon so that, as the air is released from the inside, they sink into the dye. Leave the eggs in place, checking for evenness of color until you obtain the required shade. Repeat the process, using the orange dye with the natural red and color the remaining eggs.

4 Remove the eggs from the saucepan with a spoon and drain them. Remove the pantyhose and leaves, revealing the stenciled design. Wash the eggs under cold water. You may need to blow through the center slightly to get rid of excess liquid dye. Carefully wash the end before blowing through it.

5 Thread the eggs onto the piece of wire, alternating purple and orange and evenly spacing the sizes, leaf patterns, and color shades. Twist the wire ends together, being careful not to crush the eggs. Cut off any excess wire.

6 Arrange the eggs so that all the leaf shapes are facing the front. Put a dab of the glue between each egg in order to stabilize the wreath, and then leave it to dry. Wind the white feather wands between each egg, so that they alternate facing inward and outward. Next, take the smaller feathers and stick two in place opposite each white feather. Allow the glue to dry thoroughly before displaying the wreath.

GARDEN
CHANDELIER

THIS CHARMING LITTLE chandelier, with its pretty glass beads threaded sparsely onto old copper wire, will add a magical touch to your garden decorations. Suspend it from an arbor or rose arch to catch the morning sun, or perhaps from the branch of a tree to twinkle over candles lighting a summer evening outdoor supper. For a more festive occasion, a really stunning effect could be created by making a few and suspending them around the garden. You could add tiny bells, at the base of the beads beneath the copper leaves, that will tinkle in a gentle breeze.

The copper leaves are quick and easy to make. You can cut the thin metal foil with scissors, and use the clever technique of marking the leaf veins with a dressmaker's tracing wheel. Making an embossed pattern on the reverse side helps the metal reflect the light, which enhances its fairytale quality.

LEFT AND BELOW: Hang this chandelier in a place where it will twirl gently in the breeze and where the sunlight can reflect off the glass beads.

MATERIALS

Roll of copper wire ¹⁄₁₆in (1.5mm) thick

Wirecutters

Small amount of copper wire for binding, ¹⁄₅₂in (0.5mm) thick

Fine copper wire for threading beads

100 assorted glass beads with holes large enough to thread onto the wire, plus five tiny beads

Epoxy glue

Card to make leaf templates

Copper foil ¹⁄₆₄in (0.1mm) thick

Ballpoint pen

Scissors

Tracing wheel

Yielding surface for cutting on, such as an old telephone directory

Darning needle

Pliers

HOW TO MAKE A GARDEN CHANDELIER

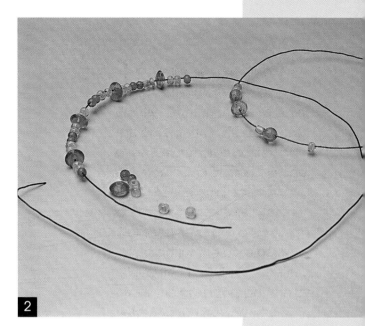

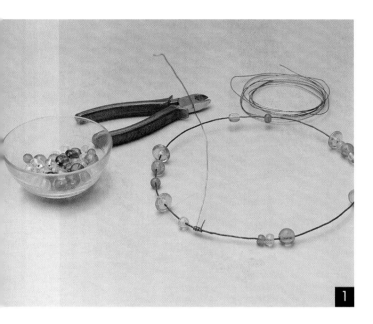

1 Cut a 31in (80cm) length of the thicker copper wire and bend it into a circle. Thread five groups of three beads on to it. Overlap the ends by ¾in (2cm) and bind them tightly together with the thinner wire.

2 Cut another length of the thicker wire 51in (130cm) long. Thread it with five matching sets of seven beads each, consisting of three smaller beads on either side of a more prominent, larger one.

3 Attach one end of this wire to the circle, bending the wire around tightly to secure it. Make a loop containing the first set of beads, then attach it to the circle by bending it over twice, about one-fifth of the way around the circle. Repeat with another four equidistant loops to complete the circle, remembering to push each set of beads into each loop.

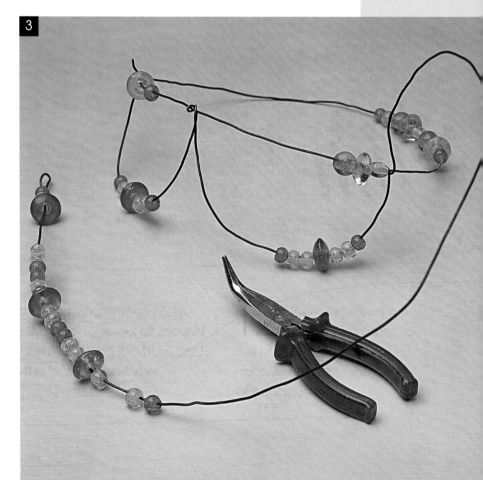

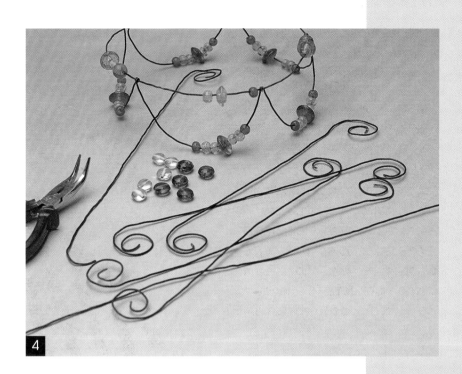

4 Cut five 24in (60cm) lengths of the same wire and curl each end into fairly loose spirals, both pointing the same way.

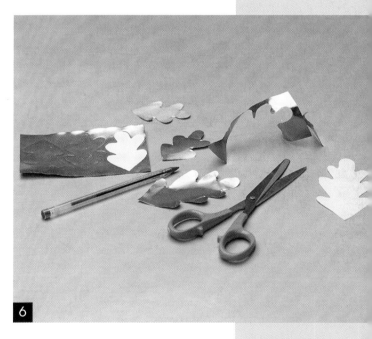

5 Push a bead onto each end of the spiral, in this case clear glass for the base and blue for the top. If the bead only loosely fits onto the wire, secure it with a very small amount of epoxy glue. Now link each spiral between the loops around the circular frame. Bind the top spirals together and insert a length of wire at that point in order to suspend the chandelier.

6 Draw two leaf shapes on card, one small and one large, and cut them out. Lay the templates onto the copper foil and draw around them with the pen, making an impression in the metal. Cut them out with the scissors. You will need five small leaves and one large.

7 Lay the leaves on a telephone directory and roll the tracing wheel over the copper foil to make the leaf veins You will need to press firmly. Turn them over to reveal the embossed side.

8 Make a hole in each end of the leaves with a darning needle. At the top of the large leaf, thread an 18in (45cm) length of the thinnest jewelry wire through the hole, bending it double at that point. Thread twelve beads onto the doubled wire, leaving the two ends free. Do the same with the smaller beads, threading only three this time. You will need the two ends to be at least 5cm (2in) long. To attach the beads at the base of the leaves, first thread a tiny bead into the middle of the length, bend the wire in half and thread two beads onto the doubled wire. Push one end through the hole in the leaf and twist the two ends tightly together to secure the beads. Cut off the excess wire and bend it back neatly.

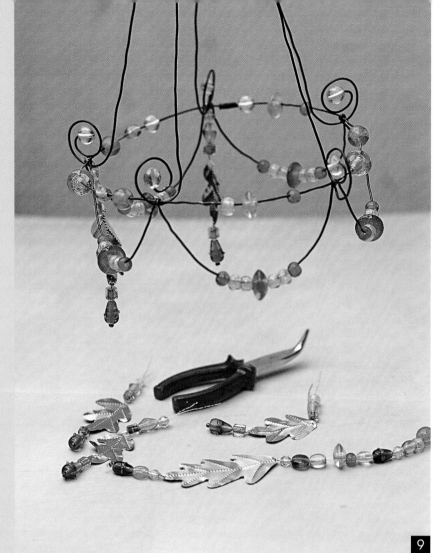

9 Attach the smaller leaves between the loops under the spirals by twisting the two ends of wire tightly together and cutting off any excess. Attach the larger leaf in the same way – to the top where the blue-ended spirals meet.

LEFT: This chandelier could also be used indoors – suspend it above a dining table and set candles beneath it. The flames will be reflected in the glass beads and the metallic leaves.

F O X
BIRD SCARER

MATERIALS

Sheet aluminum ½in (0.5mm) thick,
   32 x 16in (80 x 40cm)
Paper template
Masking tape
Black indelible marker pen
Heavy duty scissors
Protective gloves
Hammer
Hole puncher, ⅝in (16mm) in diameter
Sandpaper for use on metal
Fast-setting epoxy resin glue
Glass marble, approximately ¾in (2cm)
   in diameter
Dowel ⅝in (16mm) in diameter,
   20in (50cm) long
Tenon saw
Matte black exterior paint
Paintbrush

ANYONE WHO HAS ever grown their own vegetables will understand the vital importance of keeping large garden birds from feasting on your newly planted crops. Little is more devastating than to find that all the time, work, and anticipation that has gone into sowing, thinning out, and growing your prized flowers and crops has come to nothing, and all you have left are their bare stalks. Something must be done! This silhouette fox with his glittering eye really does work. No bird would risk stealing a cauliflower with a fox stealthily stalking the perimeter of the vegetable bed.

Although the fox is made from sheet aluminum, it is also possible to cut it from exterior plywood that is coated with an exterior varnish before it is painted. Why not be really fox-friendly and make two, one at either end of the garden, to keep the feathered cauliflower thieves away!

RIGHT: Use this outline of the fox as a template for the project. You can photocopy the image, enlarging it to the required size.

HOW TO MAKE A FOX BIRD SCARER

1 Enlarge the shape on the previous page on a photocopier to the required size – this one is roughly 29in (73cm) from front paw to tip of tail. Lay the template onto the metal side, which is covered with a protective film. Secure with masking tape and draw around the fox with the pen.

2 Using heavy duty scissors, cut out the shape carefully, following all the guidelines. You may wish to wear protective gloves, as the metal can be sharp. The scissors, which should be kept for this sort of work, won't cut sheet metal thicker than 1/32in (0.5mm); for that, you would need to use tin snips.

3 Using the hammer, gently tap all around the cut edges to flatten the outline. This also makes it safer to handle.

4 Make a hole through the metal for the eye by banging the hole-puncher very hard with the hammer. If you don't have a strong work bench, do this on a hard surface such as a doorstep. The rim of the hole will be indented inward, which makes a convenient well in which to place the glass eye.

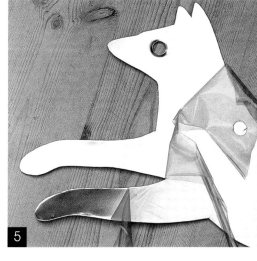

5 Pull off the protective film to reveal the shiny metal beneath.

6 Thoroughly sand both sides of the metal to make it rough enough to absorb the paint. Be careful when sanding the edges – they may be sharp.

7

7 Mix up the epoxy resin. Lay the eye in the well and hold it in place with two strips of masking tape. Turn the fox over and apply the glue all around the space between the glass and metal. Make sure you don't cover the back of the eye with glue, as the light needs to be able to shine through the hole.

8 Allow the glue to set and remove tape. Saw a slit 3in (7.5cm) down one end of the dowel. Sand each side of the slit to make a softened edge. Use more glue to secure the fox in place. Allow the glue to set.

8

9 Paint both the fox and the dowel with two coats of the matte black paint, allowing them to dry thoroughly between coats.

RIGHT: Set the fox in the corner of a vegetable bed to scare away birds and to protect your harvest.

PAINTED
FLOWERPOTS

WHEN DECORATING an object like a flowerpot, it is important to remember that the design must not be too complicated, as this would detract from the beauty of the flowers which are to be planted in it. The pattern can be striking, but should complement the color and shape of the plant intended for the pot.

Nothing could be simpler than this bold gray and white design, with its curved pattern simply combed into the newly-painted gray stripes. This approach works best on tall, slim pots or a clay pot without a rim, but could be applied to any shape as long as the pot is very clean. A permeable water-based paint is best, as it will allow the pot to breathe.

MATERIALS

Clean terra-cotta flowerpot – this one is
   6½in (16cm) high and 6in (15cm) in
   diameter, but use any sizes you can find

Water-based permeable emulsion paint in gray
   and white (this is an old-fashioned paint
   which is becoming easier to find but
   ordinary household emulsion will do)

Round 1in (2.5cm) artist's brush

2 glass jars

Pencil

Tape measure or ruler

Section of a decorator's rubber comb
   ¾in (2cm) wide (these are available from
   good art shops)

LEFT AND ABOVE: Flowering geraniums are the ideal plants for painted pots such as these, as they do not require too much water. Constantly soaking the decorated pot with water could adversely affect the paint finish.

HOW TO MAKE PAINTED FLOWERPOTS

1 Make sure that the pot is either new or scrubbed clean and thoroughly dry. Coat it evenly with two coats of white paint, allowing each coat to dry.

2 Turn the pot upside down and, using the pencil and a tape measure or ruler, make eight equidistant marks around the base of the pot. These are your guide marks for painting the stripes. Paint one gray stripe quickly and evenly down one side.

3 While the paint is still wet, starting at the top, drag the comb down the gray stripe in a wavy action to make the curvy line. Don't be too timid – the line will look better if it is drawn with confidence.

4 Continue around the pot in the same way, "combing" each stripe immediately after it is painted. Allow the paint to dry fully before planting anything inside it.

BIRD
FEEDER

RIGHT: Hang this bird feeder near a window, so you can watch the birds that visit. The chicken wire sides will discourage larger birds or squirrels from stealing the food.

ONE OF THE PLEASURES OF GARDENING is the fact that you are outside at all times of the year and in all seasons. You can't help but notice the natural world about you, especially the birds that share our gardens. We see migrating species come and go, their arrival marking the seasons – for instance, the coming of swallows usually indicates the start of summer. The gardener's friend, the robin, stays faithful to his territory, knowing that plenty of food will be provided by the digging of soil and the turning of the compost heap. But in the darkest days of winter, when food is scarce, we can supplement these small birds' diet by putting out wild bird food for them. The feeding place must be far away from cats, so this suspended, thatched, bird feeder is ideal. Use either willow or hazel wood for the best result.

MATERIALS

Saucer 5½in (14cm) in diameter, to use as a template
Pencil
Piece of ⅒in (18mm) exterior plywood 14 x 10in (35 x 25cm)
Jigsaw
Sheet of medium grade sandpaper
Blue exterior timber paint
Paintbrush
Cordless drill with ⅛in (2mm) bit
Wirecutters
1 yard (1m) ¼in (6mm) copper wire
Pliers
4 willow or hazel rods, ¾in (2cm) in diameter
    and 8in (20cm) long
Willow or hazel rods, ¾in (2cm) in diameter and
    47in (120cm) total length
Strong craft knife
Pruning saw
Galvanized nails,1¼ and 1½in (3 and 4cm) long
Pin hammer
Small gauge chicken wire, 8 x 14in (20 x 36cm)
Besom broom
Scissors
Wood glue

6 Drill and nail on the other three willow pieces over the wire on the base disc. The last piece should cover the join of the chicken wire. Push the top disc with the hanging wire attached into the same position as the base disc, and drill and nail them in place as before.

7 You now need to fill in the area between the upright rods with the small pieces. Use a longer nail on every alternate piece, leaving the nail to protrude about ½in (1cm).

8 Unwind the makers' wire that binds the brush of the besom broom. Trim this to about 12in (30cm) long, cutting away the more obvious sticks, and keeping material more suited to thatching. Bunch the thicker ends around the top wire loop, apply glue liberally to the cut ends, and bind them together tightly (so that the roof holds) with part of the copper wire. Splay the other ends evenly out over the top disc and secure them by binding the remaining wire over the thatch and around protruding nails. Finish by trimming the edge of the thatch with scissors.

D R I F T W O O D
BENCH

THIS SIMPLE MODERN WOODEN BENCH requires absolutely no carpentry skills in its construction as there are no nails, screws, or any complicated joints to discourage you. Two hardwoods have been used: an old worn elm board makes the seat, and is placed on stacks of oak blocks cut from discarded gate posts. All this is from wood that may have been destined for the fire or wasted on a wood pile. The chalky bleached effect is obtained simply by painting a pale watery blue over white, which is then distressed by sanding with coarse sandpaper. Elm is very sensitive and will buckle in wet conditions, and so either bring it indoors when it rains or just leave it on a covered porch patio. However, if you require an entirely weatherproof bench, use oak for both the seat and posts, and paint it with oil-based outdoor paint as a finish.

LEFT AND BELOW: Solid and handsome, this simple-to-construct bench makes good use of old pieces of wood. The distressed paint finish blends perfectly with the existing natural elements.

MATERIALS

Oak posts between 4½ and 6in
(12.5 and 15cm) square –
you will need a total length of
approx 13ft (4m)

Measuring tape

Sharp hand saw

Elm or oak board approx
14 x 60in (35 x 150cm)

Oil-based paint in pale blue
and white

Paintbrush

Coarse sandpaper

Dust mask

HOW TO MAKE A DRIFTWOOD BENCH

1 Measure the oak posts into 12in (30cm) lengths, and cut them neatly with the sharp saw. You need twelve in all, but it does not matter if the widths are not uniform, as some variation adds interest to the design.

2 Cut the ends of the elm or oak board at right angles so they are straight and the board is 60in (150cm) long.

3 Paint all the blocks and the board roughly with the white paint and allow them to dry thoroughly. Now repeat the painting process using the pale blue, again painting roughly to allow some of the white to show through. Leave the wood to dry thoroughly.

4

4 Sand each block firmly on all sides, and the ends, with the rough sandpaper. The aim is to create a distressed look by allowing the white undercoat and patches of the wood to show through. Repeat with the board. Wear a dust mask to avoid breathing the fine dust.

5 Make two piles of oak blocks, each comprising six blocks stacked alternately so that each layer bridges the previous one. The outer edge of each pile needs to be 57in (145cm) apart. Place the elm plank across the two piles to complete the bench.

5

S H E L L
URN

THE EXTRAORDINARY THING about this unusual shell-encrusted urn is that it is impossible to tell whether it was made yesterday or a century ago. In the nineteenth century, shell work was a popular craft and amateurs made the most exquisite decorated objects – from small pictures to extravagant grottoes. The obsession was also fed by an avid interest in the natural world of the seashore – seaweed pictures were also highly favored. It was a time when naturalists traveled the world bringing back exotic specimens from far-off places, a time when, in a modest way, science inspired craft.

Many people have a treasured collection of shells they have gathered over the years, but larger quantities of similar shells are needed for a project such as this. Luckily, they are readily available from certain outlets that obtain their supplies from licensed importers. It is important, however, not to take too many from the shore without knowledge of which species are in abundance and which are at risk.

For this enchanting project, you will need patience, nimble fingers, and a well-chosen urn. Although the finished shape will be altered by the addition of the shells, it is important that it shouldn't look too lumpy. The ceramic urn chosen for this project has fluted contours, which can act as a guide for fixing the shells. Why not make the shell candles (pp84–85) as an accompaniment to light a garden supper?

LEFT AND ABOVE: You will need a large quantity of these delicate cowrie shells. The beauty of this shell urn is in the repeated design, which has its own rhythm, like the pounding of the sea.

MATERIALS
Assorted shells – black, white with
    lilac interiors, and cream cowries
Cement-based waterproof
    tile adhesive
Bowl
Palette knife
Ceramic urn 10in (25cm) high
Small paintbrush
Damp cloth

MATERIALS FOR SHELL CANDLES
Assorted clam-shaped open shells, at
    least 4in (10cm) in diameter
3 household and 3 beeswax candles
Cookie sheet
Adhesive putty
Old knife, tablespoon, saucepan
Saucer
Scissors

HOW TO MAKE A SHELL URN

Mix the cement adhesive with a small amount of water to make a stiff paste. Spread some of the paste over a small area of the urn and add a small quantity to the back of each cowrie shell before pushing it into place, following the contours of the urn.

Continue sticking similar shells in place, row by row, until the central body of the urn is completely covered. Try to be as neat as possible, using just enough adhesive to make the shells secure but not so much that it obscures a lot of the shell.

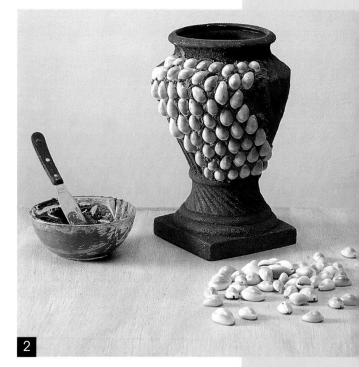

82

3

4

3 Add a row of small black shells directly above the section of cowrie shells. Repeat with a similar row at the base, and another row approximately 1¼in (3cm) below it.

4 Now fill the remaining section with the lilac-centered shells. Position them so they reveal their colored insides. Remember to spread adhesive onto the urn as well as onto the backs of the shells.

5 Stick the larger black shells around the neck of the urn, making sure that the center of the spiral is facing upward. Add a row of lilac-centered shells inside the black so that they are also facing upward. You will probably need to build up a layer of the adhesive underneath them to provide extra support.

Allow the adhesive to begin to harden, then clean off the excess adhesive around each shell, using the small brush dipped in water. When the adhesive is almost hardened, polish with a damp cloth to remove any remaining traces of it.

5

SHELL CANDLES

HOW TO MAKE SHELL CANDLES

1 Wipe the inside and outside of the shells with paper towels to ensure all surfaces are clean. Position them on a cookie sheet, placing small balls of adhesive putty underneath each shell to prevent them wobbling and, most importantly, to make them level.

2 Place beeswax and household candles in an old saucepan over a low heat and gently melt the wax. You may need to cut longer candles into pieces so they don't hang over the edge. As the wax melts, remove the released wicks and place to one side.

3 Remove the pan from the heat when the wax is completely liquid and spoon it very carefully into each shell to a depth of ¼in (5mm) from the rim. Allow the wax to begin to set.

4 Cut the wicks into short lengths and push a piece into the center of each candle, allowing about ¾in (1.5cm) to extend above the wax. The wax tends to shrink as it sets, so fill the shells to their rims with more molten wax (you may need to reheat it). Set aside and leave to cool.

WIRE
POT HOLDERS

WIRE IS A WONDERFUL MATERIAL to work with. It comes in so many colors and sizes and really lends itself to the decorative crafts. At one time, many garden objects would have been made from ornately twisted wire, such as the covetable jardinières and hanging baskets made in the nineteenth century when decorative wirework was at its height. This pretty wire pot holder pays homage to that history.

When you work a lot with wire, you begin to understand that what often appears to be a purely decorative feature is actually a structural part of the design. Here, a pliable green plastic-coated gardening wire has been used, and the design is highlighted by placing a pale-colored pot inside.

RIGHT: The decorative looped base of the wire frame keeps the pot slightly off the ground and enables the plant to drain freely.

ABOVE AND LEFT: These wire holders are ideal for containing small pots of herbs to be placed just outside the kitchen door.

MATERIALS

Roll of green plastic coated garden wire,¹⁄₁₆in (1.5mm) thick
Roll of green plastic coated garden wire, ¹⁄₃₂in (0.7mm) thick
Pale clay flowerpot, 6½in (17cm) high by 7in (18cm) wide
Wirecutters
Pliers
Cardboard tube or length of dowel approximately 1¼in (3cm) in diameter

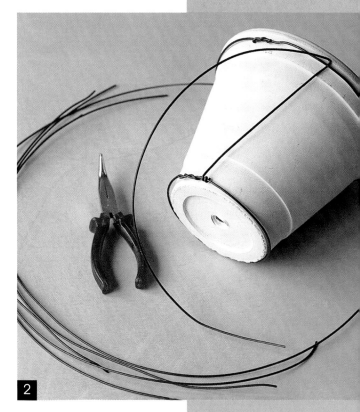

HOW TO MAKE WIRE POT HOLDERS

1 Place the pot upside down and cut two lengths of the thicker wire to make a ring around the top and one around the base. The wire should fit loosely. Cut to leave about 1¼in (3cm) extra at each end. Twist the wire ends together neatly around the pot to secure it.

2 Cut six 25½in (65cm) lengths of thicker wire. Attach one end of one wire to the base ring on the pot, bending it over twice and cutting the end off neatly. Take it up to the top ring at an angle, slot under, and bend around the top wire while the pot is still in place.

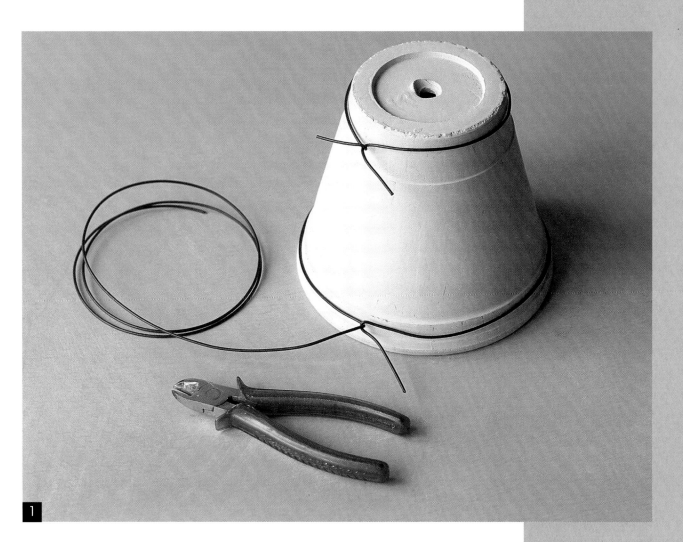

3

3 Remove the wire from the pot. Bend the wire over the top ring, and make two more equal loops in the same manner, about 1½in (4cm) apart.

4 Bring the end of the wire back diagonally across the first section, and secure it onto the base ring about 2in (5cm) away from the starting point.

4

5

5 Repeat this same process until all six pieces of wire have been used. You will need to check everything by eye and make adjustments to keep the frame even.

6 Wrap approximately 3ft (1m) of thicker wire tightly around the cardboard tube or dowel to make the loops for the base of the frame.

6

7 Remove the cardboard tube and carefully flatten the coil into separate loops. You will need approximately thirteen loops, plus ¾in (2cm) of straight wire at each end.

7

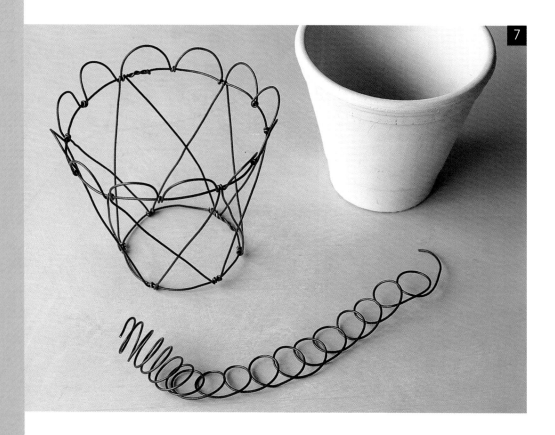

8 Using the thinner wire, bind the loops onto the base ring tightly and tuck in both ends. Bind securely and cut off the protruding ends to finish.

RIGHT: The finished wire framework can be gently manipulated to make the design even all around, and to make it fit the flowerpot snugly.

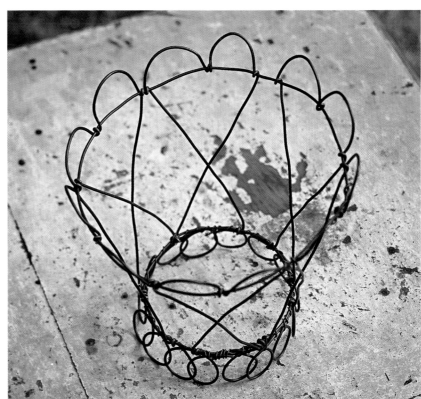

GLASS JAR
LANTERNS

ONE OF THE REAL PLEASURES of summer is the opportunity the good weather brings for dining and entertaining in your backyard. As the sun sets, there is nothing more atmospheric and calming than a cluster of flickering candles surrounding the table, or spots of candlelight dotted around the garden.

Candles used outside on a summer evening need to be protected with lanterns from even the gentlest of breezes. Jelly jars have traditionally been used for this purpose but now, with everyone's growing interest in outdoor living, it is possible to find all sorts of decorative glass candleholders.

The opaque and green-patterned glass candleholder used here has the added advantage of a well-defined rim, which makes it much easier to secure the wire when attaching the twisted handles. The length of the handles means it is quite easy to hook the lantern onto the branches of an overhanging tree or trellis.

LEFT: Several summer lanterns can be positioned around the garden, hung by their handles from branches, dotted along borders, or simply arranged in a small group to create a serene and romantic light on an outdoor wirework table.

MATERIALS

2 small pieces of sponge

Glass candleholder with rim, approximately 4½in (11cm) high with a diameter of 3¼in (8.5cm)

Vice

Roll of galvanized wire, 1⁄16in (1.25mm) thick

Wirecutters

Small reel of colored wire, 1⁄16in (0.5mm) thick

Hand drill

Small roll of galvanized wire, 1⁄24in (1mm) thick, for binding

Large green glass bead with central opening at least ¼in (5mm) in diameter

Bent-nosed pliers

Votive candle

HOW TO MAKE THE LANTERNS

Place the pieces of sponge on either side of the glass to protect it. Place the glass and the sponges into the vice and tighten extremely carefully, making sure not to use too much pressure. For each candleholder, cut two 43-in (110-cm) lengths of ¹⁄₁₆in (1.5mm) wire using the wirecutters. Place the wire around the rim of the glass and, where it meets, add a twisted 24-in (60-cm) length of the colored wire. Twist all three wires once clockwise to secure them in place.

Feed the ends of these wires into the drill chuck, tighten to secure them, then wind the drill gently until the wire is twisted to the right tension. As you are doing this, pull the wire to keep it taut, making an even twist.

3 Undo the vice and turn the glass around. Twist a second handle onto the opposite side of the glass in the same way. Trim each wire to the same length. Bring the wires together after 8in (20cm) and bind with ½₄in (1mm) wire to secure. Thread the glass bead over this join.

BELOW: These summer lanterns can also be used to protect scented candles from evening breezes. Candles scented with citronella oil are often used to repel mosquitoes.

4 Using bent-nosed pliers, turn each end into a spiral, either inward to create a heart shape, or outward to make scrolls. Bind together with ½₄in (1mm) wire. Place a votive candle in the candleholder.

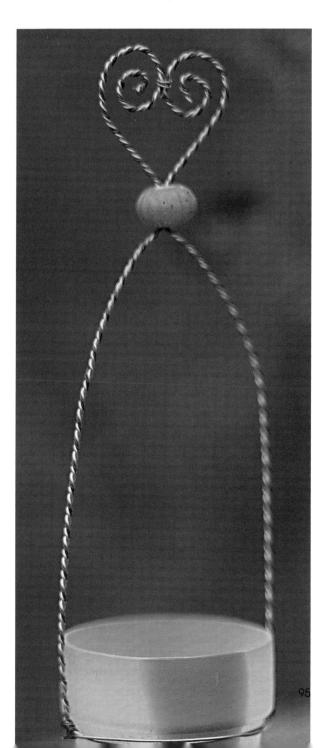

ALPHABET
PEBBLES

MANY PEOPLE COLLECT rocks or interesting stones while away from home – perhaps on a vacation by the sea or while hiking in the mountains. They act as reminders of a place and time, but they are often simply strewn around a garden in a random manner with no particular purpose.

A collection of different-colored pebbles can be a central feature in the garden and could be displayed permanently on an outdoor table. Painted with an alphabet of elegantly shaped letters, which could be used to spell many different words, they become an enduring garden game, providing a great deal of entertainment for adults and children alike. These letters have been painted with a water-based paint and so need to be protected by an exterior varnish. Alternatively, if you paint them with an oil-based paint, they will need no further protection from the elements.

MATERIALS
Large selection of smooth pebbles in
    varying sizes
Letter templates (see step 1)
Scissors
Pencil
Gouache paint (white and black)
Very fine paintbrush
Saucer, to use as a palette
Eraser
Exterior matte varnish
Varnish brush

LEFT AND RIGHT: Use these alphabet pebbles to spell out special messages or birthday greetings for visiting friends. Lay the pebbles out on a garden table or along the top of a low wall.

HOW TO MAKE ALPHABET PEBBLES

1 Trace letters from an alphabet book onto paper or print them out from a computer. Cut the letters out. Lay a letter onto a stone, hold it in place, and draw around it carefully with a pencil.

2 Mix the paint with a little water and paint very carefully between the pencil guidelines. Use white paint on a dark stone, and black on a light stone.

3 Allow the paint to dry thoroughly before rubbing away the pencil lines with the eraser. It is important to do this before varnishing the pebble.

4 Paint with two or three coats of exterior varnish, allowing each coat to dry thoroughly before adding the next.

BENTWOOD
GATE

WILLOW AND HAZEL TREES have a long history as garden features, and they need to be cleared, or cut, every six years to allow new straight growth from the branches. The resulting wood has many uses, from bean poles in the vegetable garden to fence stakes, trellises, arches, arbors, and all manner of garden furniture. Both willow and hazel are among the most adaptable and flexible of woods. Cut from hedges or woodland in late winter before the sap has fully risen, the thinner rods are immensely pliable, and can, therefore, be bent into interesting forms. This technique has been exploited in the construction of this sturdy gate, with the curves adding an unexpected elegance and symmetry to a normally rustic object and adding something special to the entrance to your garden.

LEFT AND RIGHT: The elegant curves of the bentwood gate, here shown in hazel, bring a touch of sophistication to a country garden. The measurements given here can easily be adapted to suit the size of your garden entrance.

MATERIALS

2 straight willow or hazel branches (for the outer uprights),
    2in (5cm) in diameter and 35in (90cm) long
3 willow or hazel branches (for the horizontal supports),
    1½in (4cm) in diameter and 24in (60cm) long
11 willow or hazel rods, all cut to approximately
    10ft (3m) long
Measuring tape
Pruning saw
Cordless electric drill with ⅛in (2.5mm) and
    ¼in (5mm) bits
Hammer
Four screws approximately 4in (10cm) long
Galvanized nails 2¾in (6.5cm) long
Garden clippers

HOW TO MAKE A BENTWOOD GATE

1 Mark the two upright thicker branches 35in (90cm) long and cut to size with the pruning saw. Measure the horizontal branches 24in (60cm) long and cut. You may need to make further adjustments when fixing them together.

2 Work out the best way to fit the branches together. Wood, being organic, may not be quite straight. When you are happy with the fit, drill, using the ¼in (4.5mm) bit, and screw the four corners together. The horizontal should be about 2in (5cm) in from the ends of the two verticals. The central vertical can be drilled and nailed in place to create the base frame of the gate.

3 Take the longest rod and carefully manipulate it to make it bend. It helps to stand on one end and walk halfway along it, pulling the other end toward you. Repeat this technique on the other end. When it is more pliable, place it along one of the verticals, drill, using the ⅛in (3mm) bit, and nail it firmly in place, using about five equidistant nails. Pull the rod over at the top to create a generous curve, then drill and nail down the other vertical.

4 Manipulate two more rods in the same manner. Drill and nail the thinner end of one alongside the first rod on the vertical, making a tighter curve at the top, and pulling back to cross the horizontals at the mid-point. Drill and nail the rod into place. Repeat this process with the second rod to make a matching curve adjacent to the first.

5 Turn the gate over, manip-ulate four more rods, and cut them so that they will fit into a semicircle on either side of the central horizontal rod inside the frame, connecting with the top and bottom horizontals. Drill and nail at the points where the rods connect to the frame. When adding the second semicircle on each side, you will need to make it slightly smaller, as it fits inside the first. Drill and nail each rod in place, avoiding the nails on the previous rod.

6 You now need to add the four remaining rods at either side of the frame, and to make a curve as far as the center of the middle horizontal; this time, the rod will be fixed on top of the frame. Drill and nail the rod in place. Cut off the excess with the garden clippers.

7

Add another rod alongside in the same manner and repeat on the other side to create a symmetrical pattern.

RIGHT: This rustic gate will bring a touch of the country to even the most urban garden.

TIP Always drill before nailing to prevent the rods splitting. Fit gate hinges to strong hazel posts. When bending the hazel rods, be careful that they do not spring back in your face.

PERENNIAL
PLANT FRAME

SOME PERENNIAL PLANTS can look very untidy as they grow; the larger ones tend to fall over, lose their shape, and smother other, more delicate, plants. Gardeners have devised many ingenious ways of dealing with this problem. Supporting struts are most commonly used, their untidy nature being gradually disguised by the growing plant. This dome-shaped structure, which can be made from willow or hazel, has the advantage of supporting the plant while at the same time being a pleasing form to look at early in the season before border plants have grown up. The frame shown here is relatively large; to make a smaller version, just scale down the size of the willow or hazel rods by reducing the length, and particularly the diameter, of the rods. Smaller versions are very effective at keeping rabbits off lettuces!

LEFT AND BELOW:
These woven plant frames make decorative structures in their own right, and will add interest to a bare winter garden.

MATERIALS

Four freshly cut willow or hazel rods, approx 4ft (120cm) long
    and ¾in (1.5cm) in diameter, cut from the base end of rods
About 12 thinner, more flexible, hazel rods, approx
    5ft (150cm) long, cut from the top end of rods
Pruning shears
Garden clippers
Garden wire

After you have cut the thicker wooden rods to size, manipulate them so that they become more flexible, in order to make the hoops to form the base of the frame. You can do this by standing on one end and bending the other back on itself into a curve, so long as you are patient and careful not to crack the wood. Push the hoops into soft ground to a depth of 2½in (6cm), crossing the second rod over the first at right angles.

Add the third and fourth hoops in the same way, crossing them at the top to make a frame with eight sections of the same size.

Manipulate the thinner rods as in step 1. Weave three or four lengths between the uprights to make a wide band, tucking in the ends. Depending on the rods' flexibility, you may find it easier to start the weaving backward, pushing the thicker end away from you for several weaves before returning to the flexible end, which should be woven in the opposite direction.

4 Leave a gap of about 3in (7.5cm), then weave another horizontal band as before, tucking the ends firmly in. If necessary, use a little garden wire at this point to bind the ends if you are afraid they will unravel.

5 Leave another 3in (7.5cm) gap and complete by weaving a final band, which will become smaller at the top where it weaves around the dome shape (see left).

WOODEN BASKET WITH BENTWOOD HANDLE

MATERIALS

Wooden wine or apple crate, or planks
⅜in (8mm) thick by 6½in (17cm) wide
by 90in (230cm) long

Pencil

Ruler

Hand saw

Two willow or hazel rods, freshly cut,
each 39in (1m) long and approx
⅝in (1.5cm) thick

Marking pen

Medium grade sandpaper

Adhesive tape

Pin hammer

Drill with ⅛in (2mm) bit

Clippers

Panel pins 1in (25mm) long
by ¹⁄₁₆in (1mm)

Round head galvanized nails 1⅜in
(35mm) long by ⅛in (2mm) thick

Outdoor woodstain in pale blue

Paintbrush

BASED ON A TRADITIONAL FRENCH DESIGN, this simple but substantial garden basket can be adapted for many uses in your garden, from harvesting vegetables to gathering flowers, or perhaps to carry and store small everyday tools, seed packages, gloves, binding twine, and garden clippers – the kinds of things you carry from place to place in your backyard.

This is a very inexpensive project to make, as the bentwood handle is cut from a willow or hazel tree in a wood or backyard, and the basket section is made from an old wooden wine or apple crate. Ask a friendly wine merchant or grocer if they have any to spare. One crate is more than enough to make one basket. If you are lucky enough to find more suitable wooden crates, and you have successfully made your first basket, you make like to try and make three sizes, the smallest one fitting into the next size up, and so on.

LEFT AND RIGHT: Whether used for harvesting home-grown produce or as a holder for garden implements, this simple wooden basket will soon prove invaluable.

HOW TO MAKE A WOODEN BASKET

1. Mark with a pencil and cut the planks into two pieces, each with long sides of 18½in (47cm) and short sides of 14¼in (36cm) for the sloping sides. Cut two shorter pieces for the ends, 10in (25cm) on the long side and 6½in (16cm) on the short, and one rectangular base piece 15 x 7in (38 x 18cm). Sand along the cut sides.

2. Tape the side ends of the box to hold them in place. It is a good idea to rest the basket on its bottom so that the angles are correct.

3. Carefully hammer in the panel pins to secure all the sides together. The pins will need to be about ¼in (5mm) from the edge. Use four down each side. Check on the inside as you are hammering to make sure that the panel pins are set at the right angle.

4. Sand the box all over, especially along the edges and the base where you should try to make them as flat as possible.

5. With the box upside down, nail the bottom in place, making sure that there is an even overlap all the way around.

6 Mark the center of each side. Take each length of willow or hazel rod and match the thick end of one with the thin end of the other. Place against the side of the box and drill two holes on each piece of rod and through the box ¾in (2cm) in from the rim and base. Stagger the holes slightly on each rod.

7 Hammer the larger nails through the holes, then turn the box over to reveal the inside, and firmly hammer the protruding section of nail flat against the wood.

8 Turn the basket over and gently and slowly bend the willow rod into a hoop handle, overlapping the bottom by about 4in (10cm). Press against the side and cut off excess with the garden clippers. As before, drill and nail together.

9 Paint the basket with two coats of the outdoor woodstain and allow it to dry thoroughly before using it.

TIP The handle is very sturdy, but you can extend its life and strength by coating it with a clear wood preservative.

LADY
SCARECROW

THIS RATHER BENIGN-LOOKING scarecrow can make an elegant focal point in the garden, drawing your eye into the distance. There is really no reason to make a scarecrow scary. Marauding birds will not be discouraged by a frightening expression or a disheveled appearance. What frightens them away is the possibility of a live human nearby, so shape is important and, even more, movement of some kind. This is achieved here by decorating the flat painted surface of the figure with glittering and reflective metal foil. This is easy to work, extremely durable, and retains its shine. The scarecrow form has been cut from exterior plywood. As long as you apply a number of coats of exterior varnish after painting, the figure will last indefinitely, because the aluminum foil needs no protection.

ABOVE: Use this outline of the scarecrow as a template. Scale it up onto a large piece of paper (sheets of newspaper taped together or an old roll of wallpaper would work well).

MATERIALS

½in- (12mm)-thick exterior plywood
   26 x 48in (65 x 122cm)
Template
Masking tape
Indelible black marker pen
Electric jigsaw
Medium-grade sandpaper
Wood primer
Paintbrush
Pencil
Ruler
Acrylic paint (brown, purple,
   and yellow-green)
Artist's paintbrush

FOR THE FOIL DECORATION
Roll of aluminum 1 yard x 12in
   (1m x 30cm) wide
Scissors
Yielding surface (such as a telephone
   directory)
Sewer's tracing wheel
Pinking shears
Pin hammer
Approximately 60 brass upholstery tacks

ABOVE: The metallic detail on the scarecrow's clothing will catch and reflect the sunlight, keeping marauding birds at bay.

HOW TO MAKE A LADY SCARECROW

1 Enlarge the template (see p.115) to the required size. For the size shown here, the figure is 48in (122cm) from head to toe, which corresponds to the width of standard-size plywood. Lay the template onto the wood and hold it in place with masking tape. Draw around it with the marker pen.

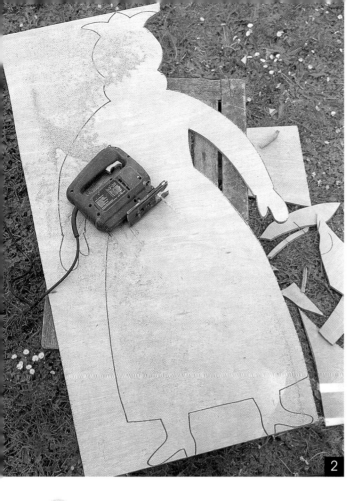

2 Cut out the figure carefully, with the jigsaw along the marked lines. It is best to go slowly and to remember to take the usual safety precautions when using electric machinery.

3 Sand the figure firmly on both sides of the sawn line until the edges are smooth. Lightly sand the flat surface.

4 Apply two coats of wood primer to both sides of the figure. Allow it to dry thoroughly between coats. Using the pencil, draw on the pattern of the dress. Do this freehand following the photo on the previous page as a guide. The striped skirt is done with a ruler.

5

6 Paint the bodice and the striped skirt with two coats of purple paint.

5 Paint the hair and crown area brown, as well as the boots. Apply two coats to make sure the color is solid, allowing it to dry between coats.

7 Fill in the areas which are yellow-green and use the black marker pen to indicate the fingers on each hand and to draw in the face. You may need to draw it faintly in pencil first, following the template on p.115. Give the scarecrow three coats of exterior varnish and allow it to dry.

HOW TO MAKE THE FOIL DECORATION

8 Using scissors, cut three strips of the foil with the scissors ⅞in (2cm) wide and the width of the roll. These will form the horizontal bodice strips. Place them on the yielding surface and roll the tracing wheel along each side. Turn them over to reveal the bobbly lines on the right side. Trim the strips to measure 2½, 3½, and 5½in (6, 9, and 14cm) in length.

9 To make the vertical slanted strips on the bodice, cut two strips 12in (30cm) long by 1¼in (3cm) wide. Cut away the edges with the pinking shears and mark the two parallel lines with the tracing wheel. Make the two curved strips that go on the skirt in the same manner, but cutting with pinking shears from a 1½in (4cm) wide strip, and marking four parallel lines. Refer to the template or the painted figure to get the right angle for the curves.

10 Cut two pieces of foil 3½in (8cm) long, and slightly larger than the width of the arm at the cuff. Lay these over the cuff area and bend over the edge of the plywood to make the guideline for cutting. Do the same with the waistband, cutting a 2in (5cm) strip, and for the base of the skirt, cutting a 1¾in (4cm) strip. Make the criss-cross pattern by wheeling the tracing wheel diagonally across the metal.

11 Cut the crown out, following the template. Decorate it with the tracing wheel all around the edge, with two parallel lines along the base and three vertical lines from the base to the three top points.

12 Carefully nail on the three cross-pieces to the bodice, using a single upholstery tack in the center of each piece.

13 Nail the slanted strips to the bodice, at the point where they cover the horizontals. Nail at the shoulders, but not at the waist. Next, nail on the curved strips on the skirt, using five equidistant tacks. Add the waistband, tacking at the point where it meets the strips underneath, as well as at the edge. Add the cuffs, base of the skirt, and crown in the same manner. Nail three tacks down the outside of each boot.

RIGHT: This rather regal scarecrow keeps a careful watch over the vegetable plot. The foil decoration, and the metallic crown, add a touch of splendor.

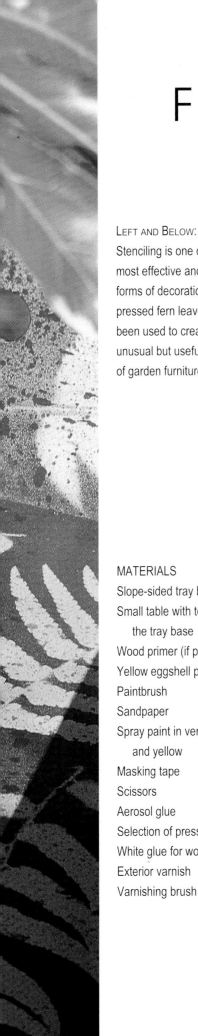

F E R N   S T E N C I L E D
TRAY TABLE

LEFT AND BELOW:
Stenciling is one of the
most effective and rapid
forms of decoration. Here
pressed fern leaves have
been used to create an
unusual but useful piece
of garden furniture.

THIS USEFUL TABLE, directly inspired by the garden, has been simply made by fixing a standard tray to a small table that is the same size as the tray. Collecting ferns was highly fashionable in the nineteenth century, and the idea of using the striking form of the fern leaf as a stencil probably arose then. It is such an exciting and rewarding technique that you may feel encouraged to decorate other pieces of furniture. There is no need to stick to the more natural autumn colors used here, although they are better to use in the garden. You can use any combination, so long as you have a dark-light contrast to display the graphic quality of the leaves.

MATERIALS
Slope-sided tray base 16 x 20in (40 x 50cm)
Small table with top slightly larger than
    the tray base
Wood primer (if painting bare wood)
Yellow eggshell paint
Paintbrush
Sandpaper
Spray paint in vermilion, burnt siena,
    and yellow
Masking tape
Scissors
Aerosol glue
Selection of pressed fern leaves
White glue for wood
Exterior varnish
Varnishing brush

HOW TO MAKE A FERN STENCILED TRAY TABLE

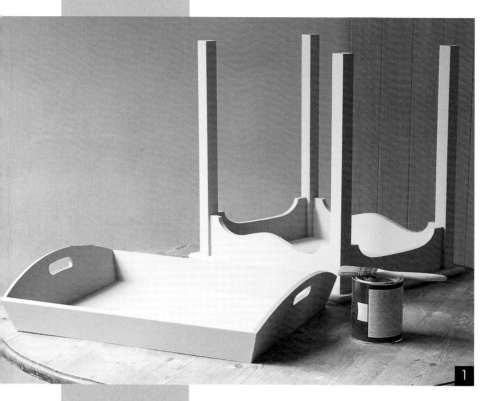

1 Prime all bare wood surfaces on the tray and the table, then give them two coats of yellow eggshell paint, sanding between each coat to ensure a smooth finish.

2 Spray the tray gently with the vermilion spray paint, pressing lightly to obtain a spatter effect. The color should be very sparsely applied.

3 Spray the siena in the same manner, in order to create a speckled effect. Allow this to dry and finish by spraying the yellow in the same way, but adding a little more color. Spray the whole table in a similar way, ending up with the siena as a speckled finish.

4 Stick masking tape over the edge of the tray and inside the handles. You may need to cut the tape to fit exactly.

TIP To press leaves, lay them carefully between the pages of a large book (a telephone directory is ideal, as the pages are slightly absorbent) and weigh them down by adding books to press them flat. The leaves should be ready to use in about a week.

5 Take some time arranging the ferns, to make an even, all-over design. When you are happy with their positions, spray the back of each leaf with the aerosol glue and press them firmly into place. Arrange the smaller leaves on the sides of the tray.

6 Spray the inside of the tray to make a mixture of fine and speckled finish. The idea is to retain a textured finish. Turn the tray over and stick more leaves on the outside slopes, and spray to cover them in the same manner.

7 When the spray paint is dry, peel off the leaves carefully to reveal the lighter color beneath. Put the leaves aside, as they can be reused.

8 Peel off the masking tape to reveal a well-defined edge.

9 Spread wood glue evenly over the table top, making sure it is not too close to the edge.

10 Place the tray carefully onto the table top and weight it in place until the glue has set. You can give the tray table two or three coats of varnish for use outdoors, but it would be sensible to store the table indoors.

ACKNOWLEDGMENTS

VERY SPECIAL THANKS are due to Heini Schneebeli for his care and attention to detail in taking the beautiful photographs in this book. My gratitude extends to my friends who have lent us their lovely gardens in which to take some of the pictures. They are Jill Patchett and Alan Du Monceau, Daniela Zimmerman and Jeremy Menuhin, Anthea Sieveking and Alan Stewart and Nan Farquharson. A special thank you to my editor Gillian Haslam, who always makes everything seem much easier than it really is, to Cindy Richards at Cico for her understanding, support, and encouragement, and lastly to Georgina Harris for her good humour and professionalism as I neared the end of this long project.